PARARESCUE

by Kim Covert

Consultant:
CMSgt Bob Holler
Air Force Special Operations Command
Pararescue Functional Manager

CAPSTONE BOOKS

an imprint of Capstone Press
Mankato, Minnesota

Capstone Books are published by Capstone Press
151 Good Counsel Drive, P. O. Box 669, Mankato, Minnesota 56002
http://www.capstone-press.com

Library of Congress Cataloging-in-Publication Data
Covert, Kim.
  U.S. Air Force special forces: pararescue/by Kim Covert.
  p. cm.—(Warfare and weapons)
  Includes bibliographical references (p.45) and index.
  Summary: An introduction to the United States Air Force pararescue units
whose mission is to help air force members whose aircraft have crashed, including
the development of the units and the equipment they use.
  ISBN 0-7368-0335-1
  1. United States. Air Force—Search and rescue operations—Juvenile literature.
2. Special forces (Military science) Juvenile literature. [1. United States. Air
Force—Search and rescue operations. 2. Special forces (Military science)] I. Title.
II. Series.
UG633.C69 2000
358.4—dc21
                                                                    99-14618
                                                                         CIP

Editorial Credits
Blake Hoena, editor; Timothy Halldin, cover designer; Linda Clavel, illustrator;
  Heidi Schoof, photo researcher

Photo Credits
Corbis/Bettmann, 39
David Bohrer, cover
Defense Visual Information Center, 4, 7, 8, 12, 15, 16, 20, 22, 24, 28, 31, 32, 36,
  39, 41, 44

**Special thanks to David Bohrer, Pulitzer Prize-winning photographer for the
Los Angeles Times, for providing the cover photo.**

Table of Contents

Features

Chapter 1

Pararescue

In September 1998, an MH-53J Pave Low III helicopter hovered over an injured mountain climber. The climber had been climbing in the Sangre de Cristo Mountain Range in Colorado. He had fallen onto a ledge that was 13,500 feet (4,115 meters) above sea level. A four-man pararescue team was dispatched from Kirtland Air Force Base (AFB), New Mexico. This team was sent to rescue the climber. The pararescue team could reach the climber much quicker than a ground rescue crew.

Upon arrival, two members of the pararescue team lowered themselves from the helicopter. They treated the climber's injuries. They put him on a stretcher and lifted the climber into

During rescues, pararescue teams sometimes travel in MH-53J Pave Low III helicopters.

the helicopter. The climber then was flown to a nearby hospital.

Pararescuemen
Pararescuemen are specially trained members of the United States Air Force (USAF). People who join the USAF are called airmen. But pararescuemen also are nicknamed PJs. This name stands for para-jumper. PJs are trained to jump from airplanes using parachutes. These large pieces of strong, light cloth allow PJs to float slowly to the ground. PJs can safely jump from planes flying a great distance above the ground.

Members of pararescue units often perform search-and-rescue missions. Their job may involve finding and helping pilots whose aircraft have crashed. PJs provide these pilots with necessary medical treatment. PJs then help bring the pilots back to safety.

PJs are trained to perform rescue missions in six different geographical environments. These areas include mountains, jungles, deserts, oceans, arctic regions, and urban settings. Arctic regions are very cold. Urban settings involve cities.

PJs are trained to rescue injured pilots.

The USAF Pacific Command is stationed at Kadena Air Base, Japan.

The aircraft PJs travel in sometimes cannot land in these areas. PJs then must parachute to crash sites. This can be dangerous. But PJs have a saying about the duties they perform. Their motto is, "These things we do that others may live." This means they perform their duties to help others.

PJ Units

The USAF has four active duty commands of pararescue units. These groups of PJs work full-time for the USAF. About half of them work in the Air Combat Command. Members of this group are stationed at Nellis AFB, Nevada, and Moody AFB, Georgia. They are assigned to helicopter units that often perform combat search-and-rescue missions. These PJs are on alert when U.S. fighter aircraft are on missions. They are prepared to rescue pilots whose aircraft crash while performing these missions.

Some PJs serve in the Pacific Command. They are stationed at Kadena Air Base in Okinawa, Japan. They work in the Pacific Ocean region. Their duties are similar to those of the Air Combat Command.

Other PJs are stationed at the Air Education and Training Command at Kirtland AFB. They train new PJs. They also provide continued training for experienced PJs.

The remaining PJs serve in the Air Force Special Operations Command (AFSOC). These PJs often perform missions with other special forces such as Navy SEALs or Army Rangers. Their missions often are classified. This means the missions are secret.

There also are units of PJs in the Air Force Reserve and Air National Guard. The majority of these PJs are not on active duty. Most attend training one weekend per month. These PJs usually carry out peacetime rescue missions. But they also may be assigned to help active PJs on their missions. The USAF even may place them on active duty during a war.

Special Operations

Pararescuemen in the AFSOC are assigned special operations missions. Most air force members are not trained to perform these duties. Special operations members may need to sneak into enemy territory. They may try to rescue U.S. soldiers in these areas.

PJs often work with combat controllers on special tactics teams (STTs). Combat controllers prepare an area for special operations teams to enter enemy territory. They set up areas for aircraft to land. They guide aircraft to these landing areas. STTs often are the first group to take part in special operations missions. The air force calls STTs its "First Force."

Parachute: PJs often use parachutes during missions

Red Robe: a sign of bravery; a PJ's duty often is dangerous.

USAF PARARESCUE

THAT OTHERS MAY LIVE

Sphere: represents the planet Earth; dark blue stands for the sky and the USAF; light blue/silver stands for USAF aircraft.

Angel: stands for protection; PJs try to rescue the injured and bring them back to safety.

Chapter 2

History of Pararescue

The first pararescue mission occurred during World War II (1939–1945). In 1943, a group of 21 men had parachuted out of their C-46 aircraft before it crashed. They landed in a remote jungle near the China-Burma border. This area of wilderness did not have any roads or trails. The only way to reach this group of men was by parachute.

Army Air Force (AAF) Lieutenant Colonel Don Fleckinger and two medical specialists volunteered for the rescue mission. They parachuted into the jungle to rescue the soldiers. The medical specialists treated injuries the men

The first pararescue mission involved soldiers who parachuted out of a C-46 airplane before it crashed.

had received. Fleckinger then led the group safely out of the jungle.

World War II

During World War II, there were many rescues by parachute in southeast Asia. These parachutists often risked their lives to save others. They flew into enemy territory to help pilots whose aircraft had crashed. They also helped soldiers who were wounded during ground battles in the jungles of Asia.

After the war, military leaders realized the importance of pararescue units. The USAF formed five official pararescue teams in 1947.

The Korean and Vietnam Wars

By 1952, the USAF had trained 45 pararescue teams. Each team had seven members. These teams performed many rescue missions during the Korean War (1950–1953). After the war, the USAF reduced the number of pararescue teams. During peacetime, the USAF needed fewer PJ teams.

PJs often used helicopters during the Vietnam War.

The USAF increased the number of pararescue teams during the Vietnam War (1954–1975). This war took place mostly in the jungles of Vietnam. PJs flew in helicopters into Vietnamese jungles. They rescued injured pilots whose aircraft had been shot down. They also rescued soldiers wounded during ground battles.

Jungle rescues were difficult. Helicopters often did not have anywhere to land. But they could hover over crash sites or wounded soldiers.

Many missions were flown during the Gulf War. PJs were prepared to rescue any pilots whose aircraft crashed.

PJs would lower themselves to the ground from helicopters. Rescue hoists would then lift injured soldiers into the helicopters. These cables often were attached to stretchers.

Jungle rescue missions also were dangerous. Enemy troops could easily spot and shoot at the helicopters as they hovered. Enemy troops also could shoot at the pararescue teams on the ground.

The armed forces used other aircraft to help support rescue missions. Airplanes often flew ahead to rescue areas. Airmen on these planes searched for injured soldiers and enemy troops. Support aircraft also flew overhead during rescues. These aircraft sent out smoke signals to hide the rescue helicopters. They also shot at approaching enemy troops.

Ten PJs who served in Vietnam received Air Force Crosses. The air force awards these medals to soldiers who show great courage in performing their duties.

The Gulf War

Pararescue teams performed many missions during the Gulf War (1991). This war started when Iraq invaded Kuwait. Iraq also threatened neighboring countries. The United States entered the conflict to help Kuwait and prevent Iraq from attacking other countries.

USAF pilots flew many missions during the Gulf War. They bombed Iraqi military locations. They also transported soldiers and supplies. PJs were prepared to save any pilots whose aircraft crashed.

Mission

Operation: Desert Storm

Date: January 21, 1991

Location: 160 miles (257 kilometers) inside the Iraqi border and 30 miles (48 kilometers) from Baghdad.

Situation: An Iraqi missile shot down a U.S. Navy F-14 Tomcat fighter plane. The two pilots on board parachuted safely from their plane. They were Lt. Jones and Lt. Slade.

Pararescue Team: A PJ team left Ar'ar Airfield, Saudi Arabia, in an MH-53J Pave Low III helicopter. They quickly flew to the crash site to rescue the two pilots.

Lt. Slade: Lt. Slade was captured by Iraqi soldiers. He was released after the war.

Lt. Jones: The helicopter crew contacted Lt. Jones over the radio and flew to his location. An enemy truck was spotted heading toward Lt. Jones. Two U.S. Air Force A-10A Thunderbolt II aircraft also were part of the search-and-rescue operation. They attacked and destroyed the truck.

Rescue: The MH-53J landed near Lt. Jones and a PJ helped him into the helicopter. This was the first rescue of a downed airman in Iraq during the Gulf War.

Mediterranean Sea

LEBAN

JORDAN

ISRAEL

Red Sea

Chapter 3

The Training Pipeline

Pararescuemen are highly qualified members of the U.S. Air Force. They must be physically and mentally fit. They need to learn many special skills. These include parachuting and treating the injured. Most airmen who volunteer for PJ training are not able to complete it.

Airmen

Men and women between 17 and 27 years old can volunteer for the USAF. They must be high school graduates and in good health.

Only men can become PJs. Congressional law does not allow women to enter ground combat specialties. These jobs may involve

PJs are trained to use parachutes.

PJs learn scuba diving skills at the Combat Divers School in Key West, Florida.

duties that are performed while under direct fire from enemy forces.

Before entering pararescue training, airmen first must pass a difficult physical test. This test includes running, swimming, and other exercises.

The Training Pipeline

Airmen who pass the physical test enter the training pipeline. Pararescue trainees attend training at eight schools throughout the country. It takes about one year for trainees to finish this program.

The first school in the pipeline is at Lackland AFB, Texas. It involves the Pararescue/Combat Control Indoctrination Course. This course consists of physical conditioning. Trainees swim, run, and lift weights during this course. They also study medicine, learn the history of PJ units, and learn about parachuting. The course is very challenging. About 70 percent of the trainees cannot finish this course.

The next two schools are the U.S. Army Airborne School and the U.S. Army Combat Divers School. Airborne School is at Fort Benning, Georgia. Trainees learn basic parachuting skills at this school. Combat Divers School is in Key West, Florida. Trainees learn how to use scuba gear for rescues in the water. Scuba stands for "self-contained underwater breathing apparatus." Combat Divers School is difficult for many trainees. PJs wearing scuba gear must be able to carry up to 170 pounds (77 kilograms) of equipment.

PJs learn how to hide from enemy forces at Basic Survival School.

Trainees then attend U.S. Navy Underwater Egress Training at Pensacola Naval Air Station (NAS), Florida. At this school, trainees learn how to escape from aircraft that are sinking in water.

Trainees then attend the USAF Basic Survival School at Fairchild AFB, Washington. They learn survival skills that help them stay alive in the wilderness. These skills include how to find food and shelter in the wilderness.

Trainees learn how to survive in jungles, woods, mountains, and other remote areas. They also learn ways to hide from enemy forces and return to safety.

The U.S. Army Military Free Fall Parachutist School is at the Yuma Proving Grounds in Arizona. At this school, trainees learn HALO parachuting skills. HALO stands for "high altitude, low opening." Some people also call this free-fall parachuting. HALO parachuting involves jumping from a plane at a high altitude. Jumpers then open their parachutes at about 3,500 feet (1,067 meters) above the ground. This method of parachuting makes it difficult for parachutists to be seen by enemy forces.

The Special Operations Combat Medic Course is next in the pipeline. Trainees go to Fort Bragg, North Carolina, for this course. They learn how to provide advanced medical treatment in this course. Trainees also learn how to evacuate injured people. It is important to move injured people away from unsafe areas. Trainees practice their skills by evacuating people who pretend to be injured.

The final school in the training pipeline is the Pararescue Recovery Specialist Course. It is taught at Kirtland AFB. Trainees in this course practice all the skills they have learned. They spend 10 days in the Pecos Mountains in New Mexico. They carry only basic survival gear. This gear may include a compass, a knife, and fire-starting equipment.

Trainees in this final course use their survival skills while moving from place to place. Trainees practice rock climbing. They go on night missions. Instructors also teach them tactics. Trainees learn how to make plans to reach a certain goal. They learn how to work together as a team. Trainees also take part in a tactical mission that lasts several days. Their goal is to find, treat, and evacuate a person pretending to be injured.

Graduates of this school earn a maroon beret. This hat shows that they then are qualified PJs. As PJs, they continue to train and improve their skills. They always need to be prepared to carry out their missions.

Military Terms

AAF – Army Air Forces

AFB – Air Force Base

AFSOC – Air Force Special Operations Command

CCT – combat controller

Clipper – dishwashing equipment in air force dining halls

HALO – high altitude, low opening parachuting

Hooyah – a word spoken by a person who agrees with what someone is saying

NAS – Naval Air Station

PJ – pararescueman

Rainbows – airmen arriving at basic training in brightly colored civilian clothing

Rotor Heads – helicopter pilots

Scuba – self-contained underwater breathing apparatus

STT – special tactics team

Training Pipeline – a one–year training program for PJs

USAF – U.S. Air Force

Chapter 4

Vehicles and Equipment

Pararescue units use standard USAF vehicles and equipment. They also may use special vehicles and equipment to help them carry out rescue missions.

Helicopters

Helicopters are the most important pararescue vehicles. Helicopters can travel in and out of areas that are difficult to reach.

The first rescue helicopters were used during World War II. These R-6A helicopters could travel 66 miles (106 kilometers) per hour. Many R-6As carried stretchers for medical evacuations.

PJs often travel in helicopters during rescues.

In 1966, the military created the HH-53 Super Jolly Green Giant helicopter. It carried as many as 15 stretchers and traveled 164 miles (264 kilometers) per hour.

In 1966, the military also designed helicopters that could refuel in the air. A tanker airplane could refuel a helicopter while both aircraft were flying. This allowed helicopters to fly farther without stopping. Pararescuemen then could reach and evacuate survivors more quickly.

Helicopters Today

Today, the MH-60G Pave Hawk is one of the main USAF rescue helicopters. This helicopter flies well at night and in bad weather. Its rescue hoist can lift three people at one time while the helicopter hovers. The MH-60G Pave Hawk can fly up to 184 miles (296 kilometers) per hour.

The MH-53J Pave Low III is another rescue helicopter. It is the largest and most powerful helicopter in the USAF. It can fly up to 165

The HH-53 Super Jolly Green Giant helicopter could be refueled in flight.

miles (266 kilometers) per hour. The MH-53J Pave Low III can carry as many as 14 stretchers.

The MH-53 J Pave Low III also has an advanced radar system. This machinery uses radio waves to locate objects. Pilots use radar systems to guide their helicopters. Pilots can fly

the MH-53J Pave Low III at night while only
100 feet (30 meters) above the ground.

Other Vehicles

The military can drop vehicles by parachute to
support pararescue units on the ground and in
the water. PJs use inflatable boats for ocean
rescues. These rubber boats fill with air. They
are dropped out of an aircraft near rescue sites.
The boats have motors to help PJs reach
survivors quickly.

The Rescue All Terrain Transport (RATT)
is a medical vehicle. It can travel over very
bumpy land. The RATT carries up to six
patients on stretchers. It also carries a driver
and three PJs.

Weapons and Equipment

Pararescue units use other special equipment
to help carry out their missions. They carry
up to 125 pounds (57 kilograms) of gear.
Their medical rucksack is one of the most
important pieces of equipment. This bag usually

**PJs sometimes use inflatable rafts dropped from
aircraft during rescues.**

holds enough medical equipment to treat about three patients.

PJs perform many rescues under enemy fire. They carry weapons for protection. One of their main weapons is the M-4 carbine. This short rifle can fire bullets rapidly. PJs also carry M-9 pistols.

PJs need other equipment to help perform their missions. PJs wear night vision goggles (NVGs) for night missions. These goggles use light from the moon and stars to help PJs see in the dark. PJs carry oxygen equipment for HALO parachuting. There is very little oxygen at high altitudes. Oxygen equipment helps PJs breathe at these altitudes. PJs also carry rappelling equipment. PJs use these ropes to climb down steep hillsides or to lower themselves from helicopters.

Important Dates

1939 – World War II begins

1943 – Lieutenant Colonel Don Fleckinger and two medical specialists parachute into the Burma jungles; they rescue 21 soldiers whose aircraft had crashed.

1947 – The USAF creates five pararescue teams

1950 – The Korean War begins; 45 PJ teams are created.

1954 – The Vietnam War begins

1966 – The U.S. military develops the HH-53 Jolly Green Giant helicopter

1966 – The U.S. military develops in-flight fueling for helicopters

1966 – PJs help rescue the Gemini 8 astronauts

1989 – Operation Just Cause; PJs use RATT vehicles to treat and evacuate injured U.S. troops in Panama.

1991 – Gulf War; a PJ team rescues Lt. Jones.

1994 – M-4 carbine rifle first used

1995 – The air force approves the CV-22 Osprey aircraft; this aircraft will be the AFSOC's aircraft of the future.

1998 – A pararescue team rescues a mountain climber in the Sangre de Cristo Mountain Range in Colorado

Chapter 5

Continuing Missions

Pararescue teams carry out humanitarian rescue missions. They perform these missions to help civilians in other countries. These people are not in the military. But they may have suffered harm because of major disasters. These disasters may include hurricanes, floods, earthquakes, or wars.

PJs also perform training missions with military members of allied countries. They train with rescue teams from Canada and many European countries. These countries share ideas to improve rescue skills.

PJs train with members of allied countries. Here, PJs train with Canadian military members.

Search and Rescue

Pararescue teams also help find and rescue civilians in trouble. PJs rescue civilians injured in climbing, boating, and airplane accidents. They also may help treat and evacuate civilians injured in storms.

Pararescue and NASA

In 1966, pararescue became part of the space program. PJs provided rescue support for space missions. PJs carried out a rescue during the Gemini 8 space flight in 1966.

The two astronauts aboard the Gemini 8 spacecraft were forced to end their mission early. Their spacecraft splashed down into the ocean. Three PJs parachuted into the ocean. They attached equipment to the spacecraft to help it float. The PJs stayed with the astronauts until a navy ship arrived three hours later.

Today, pararescue teams provide support to the space shuttle program. PJs help rescue the shuttle crew members in the case of an unplanned landing.

PJs helped rescue the Gemini 8 astronauts.

Future of Pararescue

New equipment helps pararescue teams perform their duties. The CV-22 Osprey is a tilt-rotor aircraft. It can take off and land like a helicopter. The CV-22 Osprey needs a smaller area to land than an airplane needs. But it can fly like an airplane. The CV-22 Osprey can fly farther and faster than most helicopters. The military plans to begin using the CV-22 Opsrey in the early 2000s.

The CV-22 will help PJs perform rescue missions safely and quickly. The CV-22 will be able to bring PJs into enemy areas in complete darkness. This aircraft will fly up to 342 miles (550 kilometers) per hour. Military officials expect it to replace all of the MH-53J Pave Low III and MH-60G Pave Hawk helicopters.

Some military leaders believe there will not be major wars in the future. Instead, the United States may perform more special operations missions. Pararescuemen may be needed more than ever for these missions.

A tilt-rotor aircraft flies like both an airplane and a helicopter.

Words to Know

altitude (AL-ti-tood)—the height of an object above the ground

arctic (ARK-tik)—an extremely cold and wintery area

branch (BRANCH)—one part of the U.S. military; the air force, army, marines, and navy are all branches of the U.S. military.

egress (EE-gress)—to exit or escape something; pararescuemen learn how to escape sinking aircraft during egress training.

evacuate (i-VAK-yoo-ate)—to move from an unsafe area

hoist (HOIST)—a cable to lift heavy objects

hover (HUHV-ur)—to remain in one place in the air; helicopters can hover.

mission (MISH-uhn)—a military task

motto (MOT-oh)—saying that states what a group stands for

parachute (PA-ruh-shoot)—a piece of strong fabric used to drop people and equipment safely from aircraft

radar (RAY-dar)—equipment that uses radio waves to locate objects

survivor (sur-VYE-vur)—someone who lives through an accident

tactics (TAK-tiks)—plans developed to reach a specific goal

tanker (TANG-kur)—an aircraft that carries fuel to refuel other aircraft while in flight

urban (UR-buhn)—to do with a city

To Learn More

Blue, Rose and Corinne J. Naden. *The U.S. Air Force.* Defending Our Country. Brookfield, Conn.: Millbrook Press, 1993.

Bohrer, David. *America's Special Forces.* Osceola, Wis.: MBI Publishing Co., 1998.

Green, Michael. *The United States Air Force.* Serving Your Country. Mankato, Minn.: Capstone Books, 1998.

Schleifer, Jay. *Combat Helicopters.* Wings. Minneapolis: Capstone Books, 1996.

Useful Addresses

Air Force Public Affairs Office
1690 Air Force Pentagon
Washington, DC 20330-1690

The Pararescue Association
P.O. Box 13351
Albuquerque, NM 87192-3351

Pararescue/Combat Control Selection Team
1780 Carswell Avenue, Suite 2
Lackland AFB, TX 78236-5506

United States Air Force Museum
1100 Spaatz Street
Wright-Patterson AFB
Dayton, OH 45433-7102

Internet Sites

Air Force Link
http://www.af.mil

Jim Thede's USAF Pararescue Homepage
http://www.geocities.com/Pentagon/6707

United States Air Force Pararescue Association
http://www.pjassn.org

USAF Pararescue
http://www.hurlburt.af.mil/stn/pj/index.html

USAF Special Tactics
http://www.specialtactics.com/pararescue.html

Index